STEADY, MY GAZE

STEADY, MY GAZE

POEMS BY MARIE-ELIZABETH MALI

M-EMali

*For Peter and Sarah,
So glad we're
family now!
love
Marie-Elizabeth*

TEBOT BACH • HUNTINGTON BEACH • CALIFORNIA • 2011

Cover photo: Lawrence Lawry/Photodisc/Getty Images
Author photo: Peter Dressel
Design, layout: Melanie Matheson, Rolling Rhino Communications

ISBN 13:   978-1-893670-66-2

Library of Congress Control Number: 2010941147

A Tebot Bach book

First Edition

Tebot Bach, Welsh for little teapot, is A Nonprofit Public Benefit Corporation which sponsors workshops, forums, lectures, and publications.

The Tebot Bach Mission: Advancing Literacy, Strengthening Community, and Transforming life experiences with the power of poetry through readings, workshops, and publications.

This book is made possible by a grant from The San Diego Foundation Steven R. and Lera B. Smith Fund at the recommendation of Lera Smith.

www.tebotbach.org

For Taylor

TABLE OF CONTENTS

who looks outside, dreams; who looks inside, awakens.

— Carl Gustav Jung

Above all, to watch. To try and understand. To never look away.
And never, never, to forget.

— Arundhati Roy

Hambrienta

Palabras son particulas de polvo
flotando en un rayo de luz

que divide el cuarto en dos,
un mapa de abandono.

No alcanzan. Toda mi vida
he querido tocar la chispa:

el tú que es más yo que yo,
el yo dentro de todos.

Necesito telescopio, tren,
y espejo para conocerte

pero no me llevan al fondo.
Tampoco te puedo conocer

por dichos sino por cambios
en el aire después que te has ido.

Tengo hambre. No me des
teorías ni noticias ni piropos.

Una amiga mía dice que el amor
no es sentimiento sino acción.

Extiéndeme la mano. Hagamos añicos
los ídolos que nos separan.

THE QUESTIONS THEMSELVES

Origins

I'm from the subway's roar-squeal through a sidewalk grate
I'm from sheets rustled and shoes shaken to wake snakes
I'm from Sasson jeans and *how'd a girl like you learn to dance like that*
I'm from human cactii and emotional thermoclines
I'm from marginalia and *what language is she speaking*
I'm from smoking in dunes and puking in taxis
I'm from hibiscus bougainvillea and cricket-song
I'm from DNA's loaded gun and a house in flames
I'm from wake up calls like a tire iron hitting concrete
I'm from turning *prey* into *praise*
I'm from hearts like bird feeders found by bears in spring
I'm from catcalls and hard-face
I'm from joy's footsteps getting fainter down the stairs
I'm from seeking God like the last pear on the tree in October
I'm from love like a tourniquet on the arm of a ghost

Taken for Granted

Hands leave behind more than prints—
the knitting and the ripping, empty
grape stems in a red bowl, a bruise.
When I said engine I meant death.
Grace invites us into itself so consistently
we can refuse it. Stars uncover their eyes
in the dark. Lightning always seeks
the ground. Morning will find us
still breathing. I never understood
the impulse to carve initials into a tree,
plant my footprint in wet concrete.
Forgetfulness is ecstasy's cousin.
I'd be lost without the horizon.
Nothing royal about a queen-sized bed.
Twists and turns are the most direct.
Maybe careen is my normal. I need
a mirror to see my face, and even then
it's on backwards. I'm not you. I'm like
you. I'm nothing but you. Some lotuses
only bloom in moonlight. Sound needs
silence to make sense. When I eat grapes,
I eat the sun. Inside the bruise, my song.

The Questions Themselves

Some days I'm my own private congregation.
Others, a souvenir shell. I want to believe

a dogma-free life is possible. But everywhere,
another brass horse to polish.

Where is God, really? My search began
when this world became unbearable. This word.

As a teen, the choice: drugs or God. For me: God,
driven to practice in response to the earthly
kink, the human tangle, beginner's mind a refuge.

Some believe consciousness becomes matter
by veiling itself through *36 tattvas* until we're sure
we're these separate bodies, no such thing as a God

apart. We're made of wood, fire, earth, metal, water,
according to the Chinese. The one becomes two, three,
then the ten thousand things, says the *Tao Te Ching*.

But in yogic theory we rise out of a rainbow
from red-root to green-heart to violet-crown.

Jesus—his heart in flames—saved us
from our sins, some say. Worship Him and all
will be well, all manner of things will be well.

We're machines, say scientists, any impulse
toward reverence nothing more than neurons
flickering candle-like in our lobes and folds.

The sun does not revolve around us, after all.

Theories are like wine glasses. Exposed
to pure pitch, right volume, they shatter.

What if, as we grip our glasses, drunk,
God's the one lighting the votives—

our questions, our ecstasies—trembling
a little with laughter, knowing we won't think
to look behind our eyes at the observer,

even as we witness the way morning
makes holy the surfaces it touches.

Stuck in Traffic on the Henry Hudson Parkway at Sunset

Three Orthodox men are davening on the shoulder
next to their car. Like contemplative nuns

and sadhus in caves, the net of prayer
they weave—never for themselves—

could be what keeps this world limping along.
Maybe I'm not undone by the clouds

and sunset's flame because of their diligence.
Maybe they enable me to move through my day

barely noticing hundreds of sights
that would otherwise drop me to my knees.

Subway

On the 6 train, a man sits near the tail—
leather bomber jacket, baggy jeans,

big sneakers. He looks about 40,
right eye swollen shut, splashed purple.

In his hands, a book. He raises
his good eye to meet mine—

one beat, two beats, three—and I think
of the old stories, when God would show up

on doorsteps in disguises—mendicant monk,
elderly woman, mangy dog—to test people.

If this guy rang my doorbell would I
let him in? *God bless*, he says, as I stand

to exit the train. On the platform, I turn
and stay until the train pulls away.

Atlas

From across Fifth Avenue, you watch
the faithful enter and leave St. Patrick's.
The congregation wanted you moved
when first you were unveiled—your square
Deco head and stolid gaze too reminiscent
of Fascist statuary, they said, but I think
it was your nakedness they feared—
your exaggerated musculature shouldering
the spheres. I'm glad your eyes are fixed
on that cathedral door instead of taking in
the view down the long avenue, the sky
you forever carry made heavier
by the absence of those twin towers.

History of My Body

My nose came with a family crest
granted to Bernard in Stockholm
in 1731—a virgin holding a fleur-de-lis.
The bloodline scattered, my eyes stowaways
to the U.S. among folded clothes.

At a hacienda outside Caracas, my crooked
middle finger curled around a machete and hacked
a path through the teeming to plant coffee.
My lips arrived in a burro's pack,
saddle blanket woven with strands of my hair.

The French delivered my cheekbones.
No one knows where I got my fine ass,
but my breasts come from a long line
of women made bitter by war.
My stomach speaks the language of tumors,

a language that knows no country, embedded
in helices impossible to create or destroy.
They never meant to end up in New York,
these German legs I wear, and these feet flattened
by the pursuit of some ground to call home.

Quinceañera

What I wanted most was to look
like the other girls—flawless
false lashes, gold eye shadow, red
lips, dark wavy hair and tropical
curve-hugging dresses. But my top
was a silver puff-sleeved silk thing
over a long black taffeta skirt,
my sharp Swedish cheekbones set off
by a ballerina bun wound tight.
My *quinceañera* in Caracas
and I looked like Garbo Barbie.

They swarmed together abuzz
with the criss-crossed dating scene
of Caracas teendom as I hovered
at the edge of the hive. What I wanted
was to be one of the 300 girls invited
who already knew the 300 boys. Not the one
paraded onto the dance floor and twirled
by my Papi to *That Girl.*

I wanted the boys to want me
in that Roman Catholic way—virginal,
unattainable—instead of expecting
blow jobs in the bathroom.
I hung back near the parents and watched
the *Caraqueñas*, so like the dolls
in New York I would adorn in bright dresses
and make speak in Spanish, Swedish, and English,
hoping, by some miracle, they'd understand
one another and love me back.

Trip To Angel Falls, So Named in Honor of Jimmy Angel, the White Bush Pilot

Dry season has started and the level is low.
  We travel upriver to the rust-red Churún
      by way of the wider Carrao, in a *curiara*

manned by two Pemón men. The first rapid
  we climb comes as a surprise—the sharp
      gesture downward by the rock watcher

at the prow, the oar in the water to swerve
  and slow. Watching the swing of his arm,
      the oar-brake, I wish I knew a place so well

I could climb the rush and crumble of it,
  wish I could see the rocks. I want to have
      more in common with these compact men

than *arepas* and whiskey. To them, I'm a *gringa*,
  to me, they're inscrutable and we don't,
      and won't, get past that.

I've heard they call this waterfall
  Kerepakupai-Merú. What's it like
      to haul tourists to and from it,

day after day, month after month?
  What does the river sing
      to them, what do the rocks say?

The next week, I return to pavement and glass,
  the rumble and crush of strangers,
      the concrete boulders between us.

Canaima, Venezuela

Out of the green jumble rise
    the *tepuys*—flat-topped mesas
unique to this place—sheer faces
    visible through the morning fog

as we motor downriver toward camp
    in a *curiara*. At fourteen, I came here
with my parents but all I remember
    is Jungle Rudy's exalted jazz collection,

chests filled with cassettes and LPs,
    and afternoons spent hiding with them
in the cool, church-like dark, understood
    by nobody but Billie and Nina.

Jungle Rudy came from the Netherlands
    in the '50s and never left, fighting pumas,
snakes, and scorpions for turf.
    Today, his daughters run the camp

to a salsa soundtrack, Billie and Nina's
    voices long rotted by damp.
But how did I forget these sights: the *tepuys*,
    and Salto Ángel, whose water falls so far

it turns to mist before it hits the pool,
    its drum and thunder doubled
by last night's rain? On the *curiara*,
    a huge blue dragonfly lands on my thigh,

and then I see there are two. They fly away
    still attached. As we pass acres and acres
of charred trees—camper, cigarette—the *tepuys*,
    these cathedrals of stone, hold down

their bass line of praise, and new ferns
    springing up around blackened trunks
uncurl their thin fingers toward
    the pierce, blare and high notes of the sun.

After Ten Years of Hugo Chávez

A crane stands, spindle-legged and glistening,
next to the road between the Ávila and the coast,
picks at piles of cartons and cans for food.
Cars jockey, racing toward Naiguatá.

On the road between the Ávila and the coast,
where landslides killed over fifteen thousand,
cars jockey, racing toward Naiguatá,
whiskey, and a meal at El Pobre Juan.

Where landslides killed over fifteen thousand,
a toppled NO A LAS DROGAS sign rusts.
Whiskey and a meal at El Pobre Juan
mix with salt-and-gas-laced air and reggaetón.

A toppled NO A LAS DROGAS sign rusts
beside a bronze plaque and ragged rock in the plaza.
Mixed with salt-and-gas-laced air and reggaetón:
Michael Jordan's slam dunk silhouette on a backboard.

Beside a bronze plaque and ragged rock in the plaza,
landslide survivors were told to forgive the river.
Jordan's slam dunk silhouette on a backboard
borders the barrio where cockroaches crawl into ears

of landslide survivors told to forgive the river.
They pick at piles of cartons and cans for food
by the barrio where cockroaches crawl
and a crane stands, spindle-legged and glistening.

María Lionza Speaks

The umbilical cord jelly that protects
the vessels, the butterfly in your neck,
the middle ear's dancing bones, the blossom
of lungs, each muscle fiber wrapped
in tissue, 8000 nerve endings in the clitoris—
you want to transcend all this.

I want you to seek soil, grow roots
until they tangle with everyone's.
You forget all soil is soil, all blood,
blood. Put your weapons down.
I want you to feed each other.
You pray to me for miracles.
You are the miracle.

Aguaitacamino

Night watchmen, moon junkies, the aguaitacamino
keep mouths wide in flight to catch bugs. I count seven
on our way up the hill on New Year's, the first without
Graciela, my *tía abuela*.

Some think the birds are ghosts. To imitate their call
or to kill them brings bad luck, except if by accident—
a car or bus. These mottled dun-black lumps huddle

along roads at night, invisible but for eyes reflected
in headlights, white wing-patch a flash when flushed.
Aguaitame el camino, querida Graciela, your flight silent
but for the pinion's whistle on a sharp turn.

Ain't Nobody's Business

Always the surprise when I step
on the dance floor, salsa playing,
side eyes thrown my way, tightened
hold on their men, the *why that white girl
dance so good?*, my dance partner's slow
nod, his *come on, girl, show me what you got.*

      Ain't nobody's business if I do.

They don't see Venezuela, the *clave*
keeping time behind my Swedish face,
the mix not seen in skin but groove:
tight, swift steps, hips rocked side to side,
the shimmy and roll of shoulders, damp
hair fanned out on spins, our clasped hands
high, his other hand palming the small
of my back to lead me around the slot.

      Ain't nobody's business if I do.

There's a kind of power in the invisible
when it doesn't matter if the wrapper
fits the sweet, when the ice cream's swirls
melt into one light caramel treat, *azúcar mamá*,
the honeyed sizzle beyond all language,
when the *uh uh—uh uh uh* is enough.

      Ain't nobody's business if I do.

The Helping Profession

The fat Texan who begged me
to give him a happy ending,
the addict who used my hands
to help her stay clean, the man
I prepared for his first marathon
who finished in good time without pain,
the guy who asked if he could jerk off
as I rubbed his feet, the sterile woman
who gave birth to healthy twins,
the ones never on time or who
never kept an appointment,
the Bulls bench-player who scored
a three-pointer in the finals, the ones
who didn't listen, who came back
wanting me to fix their same pains,
the one who saw God and left
to reshape her life—people ask
if I miss it, the best work
I've ever done. I'm grateful,
daily, to write at this desk, alone.

Volunteering with Rescue Workers at the Javits Center

Most of our clients can't stop
chattering, but one firefighter,
blue eyes watering, waits
until after his massage to say,

I found a foot today,
put it in a bucket,
and passed it down the pile.
What do I do with that?

I insert needles into earlobes
of another. She can't sleep;
her rescue dog refuses to eat
because there's no one to find.

A third proposes marriage, says
I'd love Miami, as I stretch his legs
and rub his back to prepare him
for twelve more hours on the pile.

You're welcome, we say
when they thank us, we
who can barely manage,
we who have seen nothing.

Oceanside, CA

Balancing on crutches in the shallows
near her mother, a girl missing her right lower leg
swings her body and falls, laughing.
Behind them, her father and brother play catch.
Up the beach, the incoming tide nibbles
a sleeping woman, another beer is opened.
A young veteran walks by with a high and tight
buzz cut and *Semper Fi* shoulder tattoo, his right leg
a prosthesis to mid-thigh. He approaches
the family, removes the prosthesis, and joins
the girl in the water. They lift shorn legs high
and smack them down. No one talks about the war.

The Diver

In this underwater world with its lobed and convoluted coral,
ferns that sway beside fields of garden eels, I float

toward a swath of bleached coral, no fish around, and ask myself,
how long before this sand is all that's left?

Back home a week later, I clip lilacs, their scent diffusing through
the room, marvel at the first open peony, its heady perfume,

and decide to leave it in the garden with the budding lilies,
all planted by the previous owners, his blindness—

second brain tumor at 36—forcing them to sell
the home they'd built to live in all their lives.

Most days I long for perfection, for everyone to be safe.
Maybe the only perfect thing in life is longing.

Praise this beautiful, terrible world where we are opened
and crushed, where the kiss comes from a mouth that bites.

O THREE-EYED LORD

Chant

I know he was just a cat, Jet Boy, but I chant
108 times—asking for his soul's liberation to be easy
as a cucumber dropping off the vine, point of attachment
scarcely marked—the Great Death-Conquering Mantra
in praise of Shiva, whose eyes open to create the universe,
destroyed when they close. All bodies hurtle toward
the exit sign. Before breaking the sound barrier,
a plane rattles as if splitting apart.

Aeolian

A cat leaves a dead mouse by the beloved's bed,
no sign of blood. Mozart's on the stereo, Aeolian scale—
natural minor, no alterations. A symphony needs
the minor keys, like sainthood needs hunger.
Even torture has been holy. What if God is the cat
who bats prey about the room and grunts with pleasure?
Or maybe we're the cat and God the one in bed
who tosses out the offered mouse with a hint of pride.

Linea Alba

Nothing is not God. *Nothing*? If true, then Abu Ghraib
guards' victims were offerings, an impulse holy
and blind. The desire to please turned river of red:
still God? How hidden the universe's linea alba.
How veiled its interstices. So many killed
in one city, one civil war—not collateral damage,
but aimed at and gunned down—the funeral home
ran out of letters to spell their names.

Waiting

All night after 9-11, we waited at Chelsea Piers
for bodies that never arrived. *Where else would I be?*
said a doctor from Argentina, on this, the first day
of her vacation. Around 4 a.m., firefighters came,
skin and eye checks required at shift's end.
Easy to view them as God, or me, their answers
mumbled, eyes on their shoes. But terrorists?
In what way are they God? In what way, me?

Blast

Pulling out of Union Square station, the subway
sounds the first three notes of *There's a place for us,
somewhere a place for us.* A woman sits on me, shoves
her dim planet-face at mine and blames me
for not moving. My face half numb—
post-root canal. I want to incinerate her
with a blast from Shiva's third eye. But she
is Shiva, too. Give me back the luxury of blame.

Alley of Rape

How to walk through the world as if it's me
when radio broadcasts incite Hutu to kill Tutsi
like roaches. How to see others as myself and forgive
like the woman who cooked dinner for the neighbor
who killed her family. Three men dragged my friend
into a Brooklyn alley and raped her. Is my heart
wide enough for this? To know the guiding hand's
absence, no plan, God one with the careen.

Mantra

When my great-aunt dies two weeks after Jet Boy
and I can't fly to Caracas for her burial, I chant
108 times—the same mantra—asking for
her soul's liberation, her photo on the altar
next to my cat's ashes, though their deaths
aren't equivalent. When a plane going supersonic
rattles, strapped-in passengers white-knuckle
armrests and hope bolts will hold.

I CELEBRATE THE HUSBAND

Animal-Subliminal

I want a thousand-gallon-drum body, instead of the ocean squeezed
into this dimpled thimble, my animal small-curled in its tip.

She goes limp when restrained, a learned response, like lying
on the couch at 15, eyes on the rafters, pinned by the guy who tore

her open like an envelope. Limp, like that. Learned, like that.
My animal can't be trusted—did she ask for it? Maybe she knew no other

way to be beautiful, caged and kept, as she was, away from her sharp snarl.
But a body can't deny its animal; digestion doesn't happen without a center.

How to hold the ocean when the vessel leaks? Rise your wild,
dear animal, your feral panting my bruised hallelujah's necessary air.

Steady, My Gaze

This female body, bound
by want and hunt, rotting
flophouse, movable casket.

Bleeding, I run. A storm gathers.
Lightning antlers to the sea, trees
shudder leaves to the ground.

I will lock racks with God.
Find yourself another
woman to wound.

What man doesn't wreck
fights for each breath
until God finishes the job.

Ex

You were oxygen mask to my underwater,
a beauty parade of breath and light.
Your betrayal smacked me like a jellyfish
to the chest. Welts vined their way up
around my neck, a noose on fire.

You were the target I'd aimed for
all my life until you transformed
into blood-musket fired at close range,
my heart a lavish fireworks display
of regret flung in six directions.

You were the thermal in which I rose
in slow, wide circles, before gale force
and rain like a million tiny darts,
before hard-flap, free-fall and smash,
my wings useless in the face of you.

A Crooked Climb Toward Marriage

To have a stranger's fingers thrust
inside for the last time.

To endure the wait, learn *no*.

To pleasure myself in New York
at 7:00 and find out a wet dream
woke my lover in L.A. at 4:00.

What does it mean to say love
is God's secret name?

Like a headlight and bumper
dangling on the median after
the crash, this love.

The shock of unveiling.
To know this time I'll stay.

Strike Anywhere

When I say I love you, I mean you
are the Cyclone in my Coney Island,
the hirsute giant in my tent, my snakeskin boy.

When you say I love you, you mean you place
your heart on a dartboard, let me take ten throws.

I mean I hand you a shotgun
and toss my clay pigeon heart in the air.

I mean hot coals and bare feet, a day
at the beach, no sunscreen.

You mean every time I swing the mallet,
the bell clangs and I win another pink rabbit.

You mean you can catch every ball
thrown from any angle, at any speed.

When I say I love you, I mean I built you
a raft out of matches and hair, lay down
on it naked, and handed you the strike pad.

Rebecca

The week before marrying your husband,
I wake up thinking about you. About the time
two days after you died—a year and a half ago—
I heard you say you freed him, and I replied
that you tied him to you forever. But the dead
know better, possessed of a longer view.

We don't live across the street from each other anymore,
moved as soon as we could sell our apartments.
I still choose other streets, sure that the stain
from your head on the sidewalk
is there with your wedding photo, lilies, and candles.

Why didn't you leave him a note, save him
a year of waiting, hoping to find one in a jacket, a book?

My doorman said your body's impact woke
the first three floors. Why did you wear
those high heels? What did you think
as you climbed out in them and let go?

Rebecca, meaning *bound*, I never knew
what a popular name it is, Rebeccas serving us
at cafés, teaching yoga, sitting next to me
in class, catering a wedding, singing. A trail
of skinny women resembling you, Rebecca,
hair wound in tight knots, hands outstretched.

Newly Wed

To open myself to my husband I have to
remember he is not the man who raped me
nor the men who have tried.

He is not the man who washed my mother's mouth
out with soap that time she swore; nor the man
who lit his wife on fire, the dowry not enough;

nor the man who sent his wife back because she
was not a virgin. He is the man I have chosen,
the one to whom I willingly offered my name.

He will not demand that I walk behind him, or deny me
my right to drive or vote. He is the man I choose
each day, the one I allow into my dark corners,

the man for whom I once stripped
and felt powerful doing it. He is not the man
who talks over me in public. Okay, sometimes

he talks over me in public. Though my instincts
tell me to run—run for my life—I choose
this naked man waiting for me on orange sheets.

First Year of Marriage

Love is the burning point. — Joseph Campbell

You get up from the couch to rekindle
the fire. I ask if you need a match as you

twist the newspaper into a horseshoe
and stick it between dim embers and logs.

You say no, the fire will catch.
Everyone says marriage takes work.

We do our share. We watch the paper;
in the dark night, we wait.

Missing

My heart's a birdhouse
nailed to a winter tree.

My mind's like wind chimes
in a thunderstorm. I'm falling

in love with the lint roller
because it sticks to me.

When you're gone, life tastes
rusty like a bitten cheek.

Possessions

After the first night in our new bed,
my husband surprises me, saying

he's glad to finally share a bed with me
where I've never fucked anybody else.

When we first moved in, my bed came along.
His first wife kept their bed for two years

after they split up, until her suicide.
No way was I letting *that* bed in our house.

His other bed was too soft and oozed
his young lover. After sleeping there,

my back hurt. He ditched that bed, too,
but never said a word before about lying

in mine—never seemed to notice
how people linger in things.

Second Year of Marriage

Over breakfast and the staggering waft
of jasmine tea and pesto eggs, you say

if it were your job to create the senses,
you would have forgotten smell.

I keep my mouth shut, look
intrigued. A link to the limbic,

the olfactory: the pulse-quickening
scent—coffee, green-humid air, exhaust—

of the airport in Venezuela—or the way
the geranium in my living room sends me

straight back to my grandparents' deck,
those summer lunches. Last year,

I would have tried to convince you
of smell's virtues. Instead, I let it be.

Later, we fight over the best way to unlock
the car. No matter. Your scent, that wordless

telegram, still takes me apart, like it did
when it first arrived out of nowhere.

Bloodline

One of my parents was salt, the other ice.
In the night I'd wake choking, surrounded by water.

One of my parents was a cane, the other a husk.
One was a wing, the other a needle.

The eyes tattooed on my shoulder blades
can't stop looking backwards for answers.

One of my parents was swing, the other foxtrot.
How they twirled. I crouched in a corner and watched.

Today, one of my parents is wind, the other a deer.
I follow behind to make sure wolves don't sink

teeth into her spine, once ramrod, and now,
after what seems like one quick blink, so bowed.

Elegy

I'm sorry I didn't spend more time
with your body. I'm sorry not to have stripped
and washed you myself, not to have oiled
your sunken face and chest, your flat feet,
your swelled belly and catheterized penis
before you went off to the crematorium.
I had but a few minutes to hold your hand,
with the crooked middle finger I share, and feel
the air, no longer passing through you, shimmer.
Two large men marched in, bundled you
in a bag. They carried you out, handing me
the navy silk pajamas I gave you for your last birthday.
Damn efficiency. You whisked out on a stretcher,
me left pressing your pajamas to my face.

A Good Night's Rest

To get a good night's rest, she used to say,
when asked why she married my grandfather.
He called her his *religion*.
They married seventeen days after they met.

When asked why she married my grandfather,
she said he pestered her non-stop,
so they married seventeen days after they met
and remained married fifty-four years.

She said he pestered her non-stop,
wondering how she'd manage if he died first.
They stayed married fifty-four years
and died together in a fire.

Wondering how she'd manage if he died first,
she was afraid of burning to death.
They died together in a fire,
her charred wheelchair by the bed.

She was afraid of burning to death,
a smoker who often nodded off,
her charred wheelchair by the bed
in the one room that burned.

A smoker who often nodded off,
she didn't start the fire—old wiring—
in the one room that burned,
where they slept in separate beds.

She didn't start the fire—old wiring.
He was found near the bedroom door—
where he crawled from his separate bed.
The man she married over fifty years ago

was found near the bedroom door.
He used to call her his *religion*,
the man she married—over fifty years—
To get a good night's rest, she always said.

I Celebrate the Husband

who carries the kindled world to our bed, the managed fire
   and cool dew with low clouds salmon-coral, our sex
a bow meeting strings, *marcato*, his *heaven-haven* arms
   all the veil I need, his tongue the host. Holy, holy, holy,
this marriage-bed of love and war and the white flag. His heart?
   No truer wheel ever rolled, steady, leather saddlebags stuffed
for the open road. I plunge greedy hands in—my green,
   my fear—and never come up empty. With him, I learn
to lean into turns, trust our weight, our burning.

Third Year of Marriage

A Frenchman in a straw hat,
his white linen shirt immaculate,

calls, *Attendez-moi*, to his friends below.
He crawls down sideways, bent in half

to hang onto the lone, low rope
strung along 120 vertiginous steps

of the Yucatan's highest pyramid
with bee-god carvings

and a treetops-for-miles view.
I look down and sway.

My husband positions himself
below and to the side of me, places

my hand on his shoulder, and says,
Let's go. We lower left to meet right

on narrow, pitted steps, in the implicit
rhythm of the intimate. I'm crazy.

If he goes, I go, but all the way
I hold onto his shoulder, steady.

Rapacious

You wanted to be a good wife,
so you tried to kill me when you wed,

locked me in the basement—no food,
water, light—because you didn't want

to scare him. But I love men
who are not mine, catch their glances

and claim them. When I dance
through your body, they grind against me

and I grind back. To you, I am forest fire
and dry wood, twister, the tidal wave

that makes villagers scramble up trees.
You fear me, your body's mortar

crumbling in the hollow places.
But you miss the point. I worship

lingam as fulcrum of the universe.
Your marriage means nothing to me.

Only God meets this hunger. You want
to know God through your husband?

Unchain me, let me climb the stairs
and live in your house.

Who Says the Ear Loves Silence

Doesn't the ear love the jangling
keys, the lock clicked open,
the beloved coming
home, and the coming
too, the *oh, God!*
Doesn't it love, love,
crave that voice. The ear—
after all—begs to dance
a malleus, incus, stapes tango
with air. The ear loves
the peculiar whoosh
of wind and thunder's holler
jangling bones caught mid-sleep
in a rocking chair. The ear
loves the knock of rain
in a drainpipe, the singing saw's
threnody in a tiled tunnel,
the all-brass band. But
the ear worries
about what it can't
hear: the traveling husband
flying, driving, eating, teaching
and in his chest
a ticking bomb.

Fourth Year of Marriage

At our hotel breakfast table you take the bananas we swiped
for snacks and make them kiss. When they start to hump

and moan, the couple at the next table staring,
I ask you to stop. Then, carefully, you lay the spooned

bananas down and tuck them in gently, napkin folded back
like a sheet. My laugh makes half the dining room turn around.

I think of your penchant for depressive wives—your heroic attempts
to cheer up the last one, and now me—how perfect the clowning

that often embarrasses, sometimes succeeds. How I hope
you'll never give up. *Shhh, you whisper, the bananas are sleeping.*

Late Summer Prayer

A hummingbird dips its beak into the hibiscus,
         all flit and hover, and I wonder how long they'll stay,
the nights already chilly. Even in winter I think of them,
         wish for long beaks, green throat-flash against the snow.

Always a shock when the first leaves turn in August,
         no preparation for the inevitable. No warning
for when all knowledge fails and it's seat-of-your-pants time,
         wing-it-like-a-migrating-hummingbird time,

illness jamming the body's easy machinery.
         Actions get rationed, only a few per day.
I didn't know where my limits were
         until they walled up in front of me.

Or maybe the limits are a door. But the knob's fallen off
         and it's dark. I have to get on my knees to find
the knob, reattach it, and open the door
         without knowing if I want what's behind it.

Whoever said it's quiet in the country hasn't heard
         the cricket-trill and crow-caw, nor the wing-whir
at the feeder. Make of my ears wings to lift me.
         Make of my heart their mirror. Whole. Rejoicing.

Nepenthe

I want to say that after we got off the phone,
I stood up and went into my husband's office
and fucked him there on the floor.
Instead, I sat and thought of you and Jonathan
a month ago walking across the wet grass,
arm in arm, into our home—
you in orange with tight striped pants,
your silver hair loose, his blue,
blue eyes and turquoise shirt.
We snapped your photo on the deck.
How many things do we do each day
without knowing it's the last time?
In the middle of the night, my husband
woke me up with his desire, the moon
a streak across the bed, and I opened, finding
my need to drink that dark, scant opiate.

To the Five-Inch Stilettos I Didn't Buy Twelve Years Ago

He wanted you more than I did. My boyfriend,
when he was five, would crawl under

his mother's table when her friends were over.
He'd slip off their high heels and stroke

their feet. They'd ooh and ahh, call him a good boy.
He'd bite his too-red lips to keep from moaning

out loud. He still bit his lips like a nervous squirrel
when we were together. He begged me to buy you,

said I'd never have to walk anywhere, just wear you
to bed with sheer black stockings, seam up the back.

Now I'm with a man who loves my feet, but
doesn't want to lick each toe while dreaming

of his mother. Yesterday, I got a pair of sky-high
strappy platforms and greeted him at the door,

a taller, sexier version of wife. Smiling, I led him
to bed and he unstrapped them one by one.

Don't be jealous, my pretty patent-leather, studded,
five-inch darlings. Wrong time, wrong man.

Knife

I pick up the knife and begin to chop, the same
knife that almost sliced off the tip of my finger
last night as I prepared soup. Another day
is another day. An oil well's gushing non-stop
in the Gulf and the *Drill, Baby, Drill* gal sends
her prayers. A fishing boat captain working
on cleanup was found today in the wheelhouse,
shot in the head, no note left for his wife.
An ayatollah in Iran blames earthquakes
on immodestly dressed women.
                              When I think
of the myriad ways there are to hurt a woman, I chop
the avocado so small it liquifies. No matter what,
you have to pick up the knife and begin again.
The oil spill washes into pelicans' nests, smothering
their young. I know some people's young I'd love to see
smothered. I shouldn't say that. I slice away layers
until only the pit remains. That indomitable pit.

Whiskers and Gristle

I believe when the chair in front of mine
bears a plaque for a man named Marshall,
my dead father's name, it's not an accident.

I believe in the white moth clinging
to a gas pump, the man playing trombone
by the highway as sunset ambers the river.

I believe in the before-sleep quiver.
The scent of rain. These complicated
brains. In whiskers and gristle.

Most days, my heart's letters fall
through a hole in the mailman's bag,
my mind a slaughterhouse.

But I believe in the rattle of gravel.
That good seltzer should hurt the back
of your throat. I believe in needling

the ear's homunculus. That joy makes
a sound bright as brass. I believe in tiny
prints of a three-toed bird in the concrete walk,

in girders and ivy's cling, in honoring
my craving for chocolate.
That the field secretly loves the plow.

I believe in the devilfish's three hearts.
The way they leave their arms
behind when they're attacked.

Fifth Year of Marriage

It didn't seem dangerous—the white dress,
the trailing red bouquet, the rose-strewn path.

The sun even broke through rain-laden clouds
to shine on my face when I spoke my vows.

The other night I told a new friend I got married
because I wanted to grow, having gone

as far as I could along the wake-up-path alone—
it's easy to think you're enlightened when no one's leaving

clothes on the floor or dishes in the sink. It didn't seem
dangerous, this decision to build ourselves a paddock

in which to nuzzle, but opening asks for much more
than flexibility—the giving up of every story

about who we are and could be, alone and together.
Marriage—this riding crop, this ground of flames.

SILENT RETREAT

Day One

At breakfast, we sit in the sun
to warm ourselves like snakes, the lawn
a star-bed of dew. At the other end
of the picnic table, a man's hands:
work-muscled, fingernails clean and short.

> *We all want to feel better, it's wired*
> *in our biology. If you're walking in shit,*
> *don't complain about the smell of your shoes.*

The sound of chewing, forks
       on plates, a screen door slamming.
A crouching woman laughs, stares
       at her shoe. Or maybe a bug in the grass.

> *You can be silent but so wrapped up*
> *in your thoughts you can't hear*
> *the wind blow through the trees.*

The lilies in the tall vase on the table
next to the teacher's plush chair
haven't opened. Will they by day seven?

Day Two

The woman in front of me, gray hair cropped
in the Zen way, tucks her feet under
her meditation bench, sits on it just so.

>   *The image you have of yourself*
>   *is unworthy because it's an image,*
>   *unreal. You interpret it to mean*
>   *you are unworthy, but it's the image*
>   *that's unworthy, not you.*

Resonant body strings, our sitting
        thrums the room.

At the back of the hall, a toilet
        flushes like a thunderclap.

After three sits in a row, the grass
        and trees shimmer. Even the stones.

YOU ARE BLISS in blue chalk
        on the blacktop path.

No apparent change in the lilies.

>   *Life sets you up for your certain defeat*
>   *so you'll surrender. If you resist*
>   *what is, you create suffering.*

Day Three

I choose the ends of rows for meditation,
tables at the edge of the dining area.

One lily open, one petal spreads wide
on another. Other buds show cracks.

> *Do not enter a war with the mind.*
> *It will go on forever, unwinnable.*

A hawk swoops across the field, chased by a crow.

The leaf-filtered light at lunch dapples
            the dining terrace. An ant walks
by my plate. Pauses. Moves on.

> *Drop the war with yourself.*
> *Just drop it.*

My heart pounds during sits, so hard
I feel it in my teeth. An opening? Fear?

Day Four

In this morning's meditation, clarity.
        I'm afraid to disappear.

            Stop trying to figure anything out.
            Stop trying to get anywhere.
            Just stop. Just sit.

Stone-marked labyrinth, one foot in front
        of the other. The path to the center
                comes near then veers
        to the outer ring before it reaches
the core. Offerings left on the central rock:
        leaves, tea bag wrappers, a dollar,
                pebbles, an eyeglass case.
        I leave a feather and turn
to make my way back to the world.

Yesterday's opened lily already droops,
        another blooms at the back of the vase.
Though what's the back, to a vase?

            Ask yourself: Do I know
            this (or anything) to be true?

Day Five

The lilies are gone, replaced by dahlias.

>*What comes, comes. What goes, goes.*
>*Find out what remains.*

Shaded by a pine tree, I sit and stare
        at patches of sky between needles
glinting like tinsel. A trail of sap marks
        the bark. I hear footsteps but don't see
anyone, my head in the tree-sky.

>*Take the backwards step.*
>*Take a break from becoming.*

A woman, heavy bag on her shoulder, struggles
to climb through the wood fence
near the dining hall. To the right of her,
facing the path she takes, an opening
through which she could have stepped.

Day Six

Next to the teacher, a statue of Manjushri,
      the Bodhisattva of Wisdom.
In his right hand, the sword of discrimination
      to sever all notions of duality.
In his left, the text of the teaching on Emptiness.

> *Ask yourself: Is it true*
> *that this awareness I'm about to search for*
> *in meditation isn't already here?*

When the wind blows, each leaf moves
in its own way.
      So, too, with people.

After a deep meditation, the sensation
      of cool water going down my throat!
        Walking! The sound of rain!

    How can I disappear
when I'm in everything and everything is in me?

> *Be radically truthful with yourself.*
> *Others don't need to know every thought*
> *that passes through your head.*
> *That's the lazy person's honesty.*

Day Seven

The same fear of disappearing
       that arose in meditation
exists in my marriage, too.

       If your dedication is to truth,
       you're never off retreat.
       There is simply life as it is.

In the same way a sock retains
       the shape of the foot it was on
after it's removed, so, too, the I.

       Enjoy yourself.

I drive home in silence, eyes
on the road, trees, clouds, sky.

EPILOGUE

Hungry

Words are dust
caught in a ray of light

dividing the room in half,
a map of abandonment.

Words stop short. All my life
I've wanted to touch the spark:

the you more me than me,
the me in everyone.

I need a telescope, train,
and mirror to know you,

but they don't take me
to the bottom. I can't know you

by what you say, but by how
the air changes after you leave.

I'm hungry. Don't give me
theories, news, nor flattery.

A friend says love
is not a feeling, it's action.

Give me your hand. Let's shatter
the idols between us.

NOTES

"Origins" was inspired by the poem of the same title by Jeffrey McDaniel.

"History of My Body" was inspired by the poem, "History of My Face," by Khaled Mattawa.

"María Lionza": María Lionza is a Venezuelan nature goddess who represents, among other things, *mestizaje:* the blending of Indigenous, African, and Spanish cultures.

"Aguaitacamino" is for my great-aunt, Graciela González Rincones Perié de Velutini (1922-2008). The aguaitacamino is a Venezuelan bird whose name means: *aguaitar* —to keep an eye on; *camino*—road.

"Ain't Nobody's Business" is a bop. The bop form was invented by Afaa Michael Weaver.

"O Three-Eyed Lord": The mantra referred to in this section is the Maha Mrityunjaya Mantra from the Yajur Veda: *Om tryambakam yajamahe sugandhim pushtivardhanam urvarukamiva bandhanan mrityor mukshiya mamritat.* Its meaning: We worship and adore you, Shiva, Three-Eyed Lord, who pervades all like a fragrance, and who sustains and nourishes all. As the ripened cucumber is severed from bondage to the creeper, so may we be liberated from attachment and death for the sake of immortality.

"Steady, My Gaze" was inspired by Frida Kahlo's painting "The Little Deer."

"Bloodline" was inspired by the poem, "Geneology," by Betsy Sholl.

"Elegy" is for my father, Marshall Anton Mundheim (1937-2000).

"Who Says the Ear Loves Silence" was inspired by the poem, "Who Says the Eye Loves Symmetry," by Patrick Rosal

"Nepenthe" is for Yamuna Zake and her husband, Jonathan Paskow (1946-2007).

"Silent Retreat": The italicized, indented texts are phrases the teacher, Adyashanti, said during the retreat.

"Hungry" is a translation of the prologue poem, "Hambrienta."

ACKNOWLEDGMENTS

Grateful acknowledgement is made to the editors of the following
print and online journals, where some of these poems have appeared,
sometimes in slightly different form or with different titles:

The Acentos Review, Canary, The Fox Chase Review, Lumina,
MiPOesias, Naugatuck River Review, November 3rd Club, OCHO,
PANK, Poet Lore, poetsespresso, Poets for Living Waters, Quercus
Review, Spindle, TIFERET: A Journal of Spiritual Literature, and Union
Station Magazine.

"Stuck in Traffic on the Henry Hudson Parkway at Sunset" appears
in the anthology, *Moments of the Soul: poems of mindfulness and medita-
tion by writers of every faith* (Spirit First, 2010).

Gracias y abrazos . . .
to all my teachers, especially Adyashanti, Laure-Anne Bosselaar,
Suzanne Gardinier, Genpo Roshi, Marie Howe, Kate Knapp Johnson,
Sally Kempton, Thomas Lux, and Jeffrey McDaniel; to the generous
readers of this manuscript: Kim Addonizio, Traci Brimhall, Stephen
Dobyns, Major Jackson, Jon Rosen, and Susan B.A. Somers-Willett; to
Mark Doty and Martín Espada for all your support; to matchmaker
extraordinaire Brendan Constantine; to my louderARTS, Acentos, and
Urbana crews; to Mifanwy Kaiser and Tebot Bach; to my parents and
entire family; and above all, to Taylor, the water in which I'm learning
to swim.

ABOUT THE AUTHOR

Marie-Elizabeth Mali is a co-curator for louderARTS: the Reading Series and the Page Meets Stage reading series, both in New York City. Before receiving her MFA from Sarah Lawrence College, she practiced Traditional Chinese Medicine. She and her husband, the poet Taylor Mali, divide their time between New York and Western MA. www.memali.com